The Power of
Positive Resistance
The Christian's Antihistamine

The Power of Positive Resistance
The Christian's Antihistamine

by
Roy H. Hicks, D.D.

HARRISON HOUSE
Tulsa, Oklahoma

7th Printing

The Power of Positive Resistance
ISBN 0-89274-294-1
Copyright © 1983 by Roy H. Hicks, D.D.
P. O. Box 4113
San Marcos, California 92069

Published by Harrison House, Inc.
P. O. Box 35035
Tulsa, OK 74153

Contents

Foreword
The Christian's Antihistamine
Introduction
 1 A Failure To Resist   5
 2 Why Don't We Resist?   9
 3 The Cause of Suffering   13
 4 Things We Must Resist   19
 5 Evil Thoughts   25
 6 Depression   35
 7 Overeating   41
 8 Pride   49
 9 Gossip   59
10 Sickness   69
11 Weak Times   77
12 Resisting In Faith   85
13 Joy, The Best Antihistamine   93
Summary
References

Foreword

We are standing on the brink of the greatest revival the world has ever known. Unprecedented numbers of new converts soon will be thronging our churches. The Body of Christ must be prepared to nurture these baby Christians. God will hold us accountable if we don't.

My good friend, Dr. Roy H. Hicks, has written a modern-day epistle which will be an invaluable resource in the days ahead in ministering the whole counsel of God to new—and more established—believers.

The Power of Positive Resistance contains the kind of practical advice Dr. Hicks is noted for. A careful study of this book will give believers a solid foundation in faith—and a well-equipped arsenal for dealing with the devil.

—Kenneth E. Hagin

As long as I have known Dr. Hicks, I have respected him for his godly wisdom and recognized him as a true gift to the Body of Christ. I have seen him continually walk in love, seeking peace and unity with all believers.

Every Christian needs to take this message to heart and apply this excellent teaching on resisting temptation and the devil. The guidelines Dr. Hicks has set forth in this book can bring you to a place of victory in your Christian experience.

—Buddy Harrison

The Christian's Antihistamine

by Pat Huddleston

The Christian's Antihistamine,
The Word of God, as such,
Can overcome the enemy,
Because its strength is much.

You must resist the devil,
As James 4:7 has said;
Submit to God, your Father,
And Satan then has fled.

Resist the idle bluffs you hear,
The lies that Satan tells.
For if you use resistance,
Obedience compels.

Our God opposes pride and sin
And those who go their way.
But He gives grace and humbleness
To those who ask each day.

"Draw near to Me," He's telling us,
"And cleanse your hands and heart,
And from the enemy you will find,
You're separate and apart."

For Satan knows the Word full well;
He flees and can't resist.
If we are humble and believe,
We can with strength insist.

With power above that Jesus gave
Unto believers here,
We have the key to victory
And can to God draw near.

He's given us the weapons
Of love and grace and power
To speak unto the devil
And his own bluff devour.

What'er the problem seems to be
That steals our love and joy,
The Word of God can overcome
And mastery employ.

If it be sickness, death, or thought,
Depression, sin, or hate,
We can resist with comfort;
Success facilitate.

Take now the armor of your God
And clothe your body well.
You'll see the sign of victory,
And you can conquer hell.

The evil powers within the world
Must bow to God above,
For He has given victory
To you, enclosed in love.

Introduction

The medical term *antihistamine* comes from the Greek word *anthistemi* which literally means "to set over against." This word, translated "withstand" (Eph. 6:13) and "resist" (James 4:7), denotes more than occasional resistance. It implies making a covenant to resist.

W. E. Vine defines *anthistemi* as "to cause to stand (against)."[1] It is the word used in 1 Peter 5:9 exhorting us to *resist* (or "stand firm against") Satan.

In 2 Timothy 3:8 this word is used when Paul describes how Jannes and Jambres *withstood* Moses. (*The Amplified New Testament* says they were "hostile to and resisted Moses.") They stood in his way to stop him.

1

The Septuagint defines the word "to resist perpetually rather than occasionally."

Christians must recognize the power of resistance and begin using it, not just for defense, but as an offensive weapon.

When the believer continually resists evil, this attitude will become fixed. His life-style will become one of resisting evil.

Let's consider a simple illustration. Tell a friend not to resist as you push against him. The slightest weight of your hand will cause him to sway. Then tell him to resist, first by leaning against the pressure you exert, and next by exerting enough pressure to push you away.

This is a physical picture of the battle going on in the spiritual realm. You win a battle in the spiritual arena the same as in the physical: by resisting.

God makes us a promise. In James 4:7 He says, *Resist the devil, and he will flee from you.* The meaning of the English word *flee* is explicit. Here are various definitions:

Thayer: "flee because of inspired fear and threatened danger."[2]

Arndt: "seek safety in flight."[3]

Liddell and Scott: "run off as quickly as possible."[4]

W. E. Vine: Our English word *fugitive* is derived from the Greek word for flee, *pheugo.*[5]

In *The New English Bible* James 4:7 is translated: "Stand up to the devil and he will turn and run."[6]

The Expositor's Greek Testament: "If you resist him, he will be vanquished and will flee from you disgraced."[7]

Here are some additional thoughts on the meaning of *resist*:

Strong: "oppose" or "withstand."[8]

Bullinger: "set one's self against, either in word or deed, or both."[9]

Ellicott: "The devil can fight, but he cannot conquer if you resist."[10]

Clarke: "Strong as he (the devil) is, God never permits him to conquer the man who continues to resist him."[11]

Lenski: "The tense, as well as the verb, implies that we can successfully withstand the devil."[12]

Whedan: "Temptations when repelled disappear, and when habitually kept at a distance, cease to exist."[13]

The key to victory and success is this: Steadfastly resist the devil. In this book you will learn how to equip yourself to take your stand against him.

— Roy H. Hicks

1
A Failure To Resist

When it comes to resisting Satan, mankind has a record of failure.

And God saw that the wickedness of man was great in the earth, and that every imagination of the thought of his heart was only evil continually.

Genesis 6:5

And thou, Solomon my son, know thou the God of thy father, and serve him with a perfect heart and with a willing mind: for the Lord searcheth all hearts, and understandeth all the imagination of the thoughts.

1 Chronicles 28:9

Because that, when they knew God, they glorified him not as God, neither were thankful; but became vain in their imaginations, and their foolish heart was darkened.

Romans 1:21

5

But let your communication be, Yea, yea; Nay, nay: for whatsoever is more than these cometh of evil.

Matthew 5:37

In these verses God is speaking to or describing people who have failed to resist Satan. Today probably ninety-nine percent of all Christians do not consistently resist the enemy. Maybe only half of them ever resist at all; the other half, occasionally. Fifty percent of the people who receive Jesus Christ as Savior backslide within the first year.

Negative Thoughts

Imagine a beautiful church filled on a Sunday morning. Picture the members of the congregation, their eyes focused on the pastor as he delivers his sermon for the day. They are apparently listening attentively.

What do you think would happen if a 3 x 4 inch TV screen appeared on each person's forehead registering his thoughts? What if a shapely young lady walked down the aisle? What do you think would show up on the foreheads of some of the men, or of the wives who were scrutinizing how well she was dressed?

If the congregation were able to read each other's minds, many people would be embarrassed! Imagine the uproar: the arguments, harsh words, even physical confrontations that might ensue as a result. (Certainly the average non-Christian would be embarrassed if a TV screen on his forehead were registering his thoughts.)

My point is this: We are all subject to unchaste or negative thoughts. Every person who claims to love God and wants to go to heaven has at some time failed to resist Satan in his thought life by entertaining jealous, envious, hateful, or critical thoughts.

All of us need to take a good dose of antihistamine by learning how to resist the enemy.

Actions Flow From Thoughts

The Word of God makes it clear that we need to resist Satan in our minds. Temptation is not sin; but when not resisted, it becomes sin. We begin to do the things our minds dwell on.

A mental picture does not focus sharply at first. It must be received and meditated on for a length of time.

Satan attacks us most strongly and successfully in our thought lives. We must learn to resist him in our minds before we can ever hope to resist him in our bodies.

2
Why Don't We Resist?

There are several reasons why Christians fail to resist negative thoughts. The main reason is that they feel protected and secure in the privacy of their imaginations. They feel free to retreat into impure and uncontrolled thinking.

Thoughts Are Enjoyable

Thoughts can be very entertaining, the best entertainment some people have. Harmless and enjoyable imagination is beneficial. People who can retreat from tension and stress into a few minutes of mental relaxation can better cope with the negative world when they reenter it.

While positive imagination can be therapeutic, negative imagination can be destructive. Imagination that seeks escape from the unpleasant world of reality into a negative fantasy environment can harm both the person engaged in it and those he influences.

Some people who have not resisted the attacks of the enemy find themselves tempted beyond control, performing the very acts they have imagined. Their actions originated in their thoughts or desires.

Attention

The hypochondriac does not resist physical symptoms because they bring him the attention and sympathy he craves. His lack of resistance reveals a sickness which is not physical but spiritual. Well-adjusted people feel no need for drawing attention to themselves.

The family's "white sheep"—the wholesome, well-adjusted member—is often ignored or taken for granted. The spiritual ''black sheep'' finds gratification from having the spotlight focused on him because of his constant complaining.

Demon Possession

Some lives are controlled by outside forces. Jesus and His disciples dealt with many people who were controlled completely by demonic forces. Mark 9:22 tells of the young boy who tried to commit suicide by throwing himself into the fire.

We hear of people committing violent acts such as mass murders for no apparent reason. These demented souls will sometimes say that ''a voice'' instructed them, even claiming it to be God.

The Church of Jesus Christ must take responsibility in dealing forcibly with demon possession. Many ministers fail to confront this problem, because they do not understand the authority they have to deal with evil spirits as Jesus did.

A Passive Stance

Anyone who has failed to resist Satan's attacks upon his mind recognizes the ugly symptoms. How can we help ourselves and others caught in this predicament?

Christians give a frightening number of excuses for not resisting Satan. These usually are based on a passive stance resulting from too many years of worldly influence.

Rather than facing reality and taking control of their lives and environment, they retreat into the imaginary realm.

A life-style of habitual failure to resist can be changed. You will learn how to deal effectively with this problem later in the book.

3
The Cause of Suffering

News reports are filled with trag-
edies too brutal to be divulged in detail.
Many atrocious crimes are committed
which never even reach the news.

It is difficult to understand how
human beings are capable of
committing hideous crimes.

Sometimes we hear wretched stories
of people being held in chains for
extended periods of time, confined for
so long that they lost all touch with
reality. We hear of little children so
horribly abused by their parents that
they are maimed for life, of wives so
cruelly treated by their husbands that
they resorted to suicide or murder.
Then there was the Jewish Holocaust,

the event which epitomized man's inhumanity to man.

The recital of the history of human suffering could go on endlessly. Why have we had at least six thousand years of misery, strife, warfare, and crime? There is only one cause of human suffering: Satan.

Satan Deceived Adam and Eve

In the Garden of Eden, Satan told Adam and Eve half-truths mixed with lies, and they fell for his deception. When they disobeyed God and ate the forbidden fruit from the tree of the knowledge of good and evil, suffering began.

Adam and Eve had perfect happiness, beautiful surroundings, a life of serenity and peace. Why didn't they resist Satan? They were deceived because they had nothing to which they could compare their blessed state. They did not trust their heavenly Father to do what was best for them. Thus, Satan's task was easier.

Today as the descendants of Adam and Eve, we often doubt rather than trust our heavenly Father. Satan is working in the same way now that he worked in the beginning. He was not resisted then, and he is not resisted now.

Many times Satan deceives well-brought-up young people into thinking they are missing something. He beguiles them into thinking he has something more desirable than what God has to offer. Failing to resist Satan, they find themselves in sin and shame.

Temporary Pleasure in Sin

Another reason why people do not resist evil is that the sinner, the fleshly man, *enjoys* what he is doing! The Bible tells us there is pleasure in sin for a season. (Heb. 11:25.)

The fleshly man enjoys his sinful activities because he knows of nothing better. His degraded life-style satisfies his carnal nature, the only nature of which he is aware.

Sensual pleasure is enjoyable, but only for a while. Its consequences, the fruit of sin, are often reaped later in disease, loneliness, rejection, or guilt.

The person who desires to satisfy his flesh by being admired by the world does not resist evil. The world admires only the man or woman at the top! It praises, adores, worships the celebrity.

At today's rock concerts thousands of screaming, frenzied youths gather to worship their "idols." Politicians, movie stars, sports figures, or other celebrities can rarely appear in public without being harassed by doting fans.

Satan promises the sun, but delivers darkness. He promises success, but ultimately delivers failure. He promises fame and fortune, but delivers bondage.

Take the Antihistamine

Second Corinthians 4:4 describes Satan as *the god of this world.* Since he already has the world under his control, he probably devotes most of his time and energy toward trying to cause trouble among Christians.

If the Church will recognize who the *real* troublemaker is and resist him, we can win the world to Jesus much faster and easier. The Church will experience fewer quarrels and splits. There will be less immoral conduct among saints and less discouragement.

Satan *can* be resisted. Otherwise, the Scriptures would not tell us to resist him. We resist him by using the Word of God and the name of Jesus.

If you take a good dose of "antihistamine" every day, the devil will flee from you and from all that pertains to you.

Resist the devil when you feel weak, depressed, discouraged, or tense. Resist him when you feel anger rising up within you, or when you feel critical, stubborn, or covetous.

4
Things We Must Resist

These six things doth the Lord hate: yea, seven are an abomination unto him:

A proud look, a lying tongue, and hands that shed innocent blood,

An heart that deviseth wicked imaginations, feet that be swift in running to mischief,

A false witness that speaketh lies, and he that soweth discord among the brethren.

Proverbs 6:16-19

This passage lists seven things God hates. **Pride is first.**

Pride is insidious, developing slowly through the years. A person knows when he has stolen, lied, lusted, or gossiped, but is often unaware when pride has crept into his life. (See Chapter 8, "Resisting Pride.")

Lying is next on the list. Through their life-styles, some parents inadvertently teach their children to lie.

When the phone rings, Mom or Dad says, "Tell whoever it is that I'm not here."

The family car may be involved in a minor accident which was the other driver's fault. Knowing that the insurance company will pay, Dad tells the auto repairman, "Go ahead and fix *all* the dents."

Children learn far more by example than by word.

Violence is third on the list. Little by little, we are being brainwashed by TV shows and motion pictures. Because the TV drama depicts the criminal as a hero, our sympathies are with him rather than on the side of the police. Movies which show our troops killing enemy soldiers are promoting death as the only way to deal with an enemy.

Defending righteousness, protecting the innocent, and destroying Hitler-like fanaticism is necessary. However, we must avoid opposing the will of our heavenly Father.

We want to hate what God hates and love what God loves. God hates sin, but He loves the sinner. God so loved the world that He gave His Son to die for it. (John 3:16.) God repeatedly instructs us to love our enemies. For these reasons we can hardly justify violence against any creature. May we all cultivate love and forgiveness which Jesus demonstrated in life and death.

Fourth, God hates a heart that devises (invents) wicked imaginations. If someone offends you, resist that flood of imagined calamities (even his death!) which could befall him. Pray for him, even if he has despitefully used you.

Fifth, the Bible names *feet that be swift in running to mischief.* This refers to people who enjoy trouble, either causing or relishing it.

The word *swift* suggests that these people enjoy this life-style. They can't wait to "spread the dirt" about others.

They quickly make any difficulty they hear about the focal point of their conversations. When listening to the newscasts, they pick out the negatives of the day and eagerly spread them to others. These people so enjoy life's negatives that they resent people around them who are positive.

Sixth, God hates the false witness. Six thousand years of horrible suffering by the innocent attest to the efficient, deadly work of the lying witness.

He that soweth discord among the brethren **is seventh and last on the list.** Church history is a record of quarrels, fights, and splits. The greatest growth of some denominations (in number of congregations) has resulted from divisions.

A few unhappy saints, sowing discord among the brethren, can cause a pastor to be removed. In a church ruled by the congregation or church board, the pastor is seldom free to preach the kind of message that will cause great commitment in giving and growing.

Don't take part in this sin within the Church. God detests it—Satan loves it.

Heed Jesus' Warnings

Jesus lists additional things we are to resist. He tells us to resist anger and turn the other cheek. He exhorts us to agree with our enemies instead of being dragged into court. He warns against the compulsion to always be right, and against the tendency toward extreme competition.

In Matthew 5:28 Jesus warns us about carnal, lustful thoughts. He says, *Whosoever looketh on a woman to lust after her hath committed adultery with her already in his heart.*

Jesus also cautioned us about allowing one member of the physical body to dominate us. An eye, a hand, or the mind might be the cause of downfall.

The list of things to resist is endless: hatred, animosity, envy, being spoiled, having to dominate the conversation, etc.

Now that you know who and what to resist, you are ready to learn how to do it.

5
Evil Thoughts

There is therefore now no condemnation to them which are in Christ Jesus, who walk not after the flesh, but after the Spirit.

For the law of the Spirit of life in Christ Jesus hath made me free from the law of sin and death.

For what the law could not do, in that it was weak through the flesh, God sending his own Son in the likeness of sinful flesh, and for sin, condemned sin in the flesh:

That the righteousness of the law might be fulfilled in us, who walk not after the flesh, but after the Spirit.

For they that are after the flesh do mind the things of the flesh; but they that are after the Spirit the things of the Spirit.

For to be carnally minded is death; but to be spiritually minded is life and peace.

Because the carnal mind is enmity against God: for it is not subject to the law of God, neither indeed can be.

So then they that are in the flesh cannot please God.

Romans 8:1-8

Such actions as stealing, committing adultery, offending one's neighbor, gossiping or putting down someone else are obviously evil.

When Jesus said, *Wherefore think ye evil in your hearts?* (Matt. 9:4), He was talking to a religious crowd. It is possible for religious-minded people to think evil.

First Corinthians 13:5, speaking of love, says it *thinketh no evil.* Evil, the opposite of good, opposes God Who is love. Totally controlling the mind is virtually impossible. (This is why people usually give up so easily when they try.) But in order to act like God, we will have to begin thinking as He thinks.

The Church must face up to this problem of evil thinking. People often say that their thoughts are not harming anyone. How wrong they are!

A closer look at what our thoughts represent might help us recognize the importance of doing something about them.

For I say, through the grace given unto me, to every man that is among you, not to think of himself more highly than he ought to think; but to think soberly, according as God hath dealt to every man the measure of faith.

Romans 12:3

The word translated "think" in the verse above is the Greek word *phroneo* from which we derive our word "pornography." Everyone recognizes that pornography begins with the thoughts. This verse literally means that no one should "over-think beyond what it behoves him to think."[14]

The Computer-like Mind

The human mind operates like a computer. It stores material which can be drawn upon whenever you desire (and sometimes when you don't desire!). You can call up a time from your past, either positive or negative, and dwell upon it to your heart's content (or to your heart's grief). The mind operates so rapidly that no computer will ever be able to match its speed.

The mind can also imagine the future—something no computer can do—and project our actions and speech. The majority of the time we ignore the positive potential of our "computer minds" with very negative results.

Examine this illustration. The first vehicle to use a muddy road makes a track. Other vehicles that follow use the same track. Eventually it becomes a deep rut.

When you think a certain way for a time, you create such "ruts" in your mind. Only by exerting a great effort will you be able to discipline your mind into making "new tracks" of thinking patterns. It takes time to "reprogram" your thought patterns from negative to positive, so don't be discouraged if good results are not immediate.

The Brain Vs. the Mind

There is a big difference between the new mind and the carnal mind referred to in the Bible. I liken them to the brain and the mind. The brain is earthy and carnal. It is part of our body and belongs to the ground where it came from and where it will return. Though it affects our eternal direction and destiny, the brain itself is not eternal. Like a computer, the brain has stored up all the negative experiences and emotions in our lives. Things we thought we had forgotten are still there to affect us as adults: the pain and frustrations from childhood, the insecurities passed on by frail parents, and any doubt or unbelief. The brain can vividly recall all the people with whom we have had bad experiences, and all the sin we have known, down to every off-color joke we have heard.

This negative brain will never voluntarily cooperate with the born-again man trying to form a new mind, a heavenly mind of the Spirit, "the mind of Christ."

The new mind must be developed until we are controlled by it instead of our carnal brain. Romans 8:7 says the old mind is the enemy of God: . . . *it is not subject to the law of God, neither indeed can be.*

Controlling the Carnal Brain

Every born-again Christian needs to

know several facts concerning the two minds:

1. The brain can bring back carnal, even vulgar, thoughts and past experiences. We must turn them aside by contradicting them with spiritual words.

2. The brain takes the initiative if we allow it. We must control it if the new mind is to function properly.

3. Sometimes the brain thinks on its own. Its ideas and thoughts would be so horrible that we would be badly embarrassed to have them revealed to those around us. Recognize what the brain is doing and resist those thoughts when presented.

4. The first thoughts you think are usually from the brain. When you meet someone for the first time, the brain may say, "I don't think I'm going to like this person." Instantly

resist that thought as being non-Christian.

Sometimes when someone utters a positive, the brain quickly suggests a negative. Counter the negative by resisting with a positive statement that represents the new man and his mind.

5. Resist quick responses, giving yourself time to think before you speak. Proverbs 30:32 says, *. . . if thou hast thought evil, lay thine hand upon thy mouth.* This verse confirms all we have seen about the unredeemed brain.

Evil thoughts surface, desiring to be spoken. Don't let your tongue say them, even if you have to physically place your hand over your mouth. Learn a great lesson from the way Joshua led the children of Israel in the seemingly impossible task of capturing the city of Jericho. Joshua did not allow them to say what they were thinking. He knew a great truth: **If left unspoken, thoughts of doubt and unbelief will not pass into the heart where faith dwells.** He made the children of Israel walk around the walls of Jericho in silence.

James 1:19 says, *Wherefore, my beloved brethren, let every man be swift to hear, slow to speak, slow to wrath.* Continually resist evil thoughts, then counter them with God's Word. Eventually you will bring every thought into captivity to the obedience of Christ. (2 Cor. 10:5.)

6
Depression

Webster's Dictionary defines *depression* as "low spirits; gloominess; dejection; sadness; a decrease in force."

Psychology defines it as an emotional condition, sometimes pathological, characterized by discouragement and a feeling of inadequacy.

Almost everyone suffers depression at some time. Most people experience it only occasionally; others, two or three times a week. For some, depression is a life-style. They are forever holding "pity parties," constantly feeling sorry for themselves.

Most people begin feeling dejected or inadequate because, in their eyes, they don't measure up when they compare themselves to their parents. When these feelings ease into their everyday lives, they become pathologically depressed.

As negativism is the opposite of positivism and discouragement the opposite of encouragement, depression is the opposite of joy or cheerfulness.

Depressed people telegraph their feelings. They spread a spirit of gloom and despair wherever they go. Some people in this mental state commit suicide or homocide.

We have a challenge. We must enable people to recognize depression as an emotional enemy which can be overcome with a good dose of the "antihistamine" of solid resistance.

Whether or not all depression finds its origin in the devil, one thing is certain: the devil will make the most of it! Satan takes advantage of our weak times, and depression opens us up to his attacks.

Turn Your Speech Against Satan

Suppose you wake up one morning and instinctively know it is going to be ''one of those days.'' This feeling could be triggered by something as simple as a lack of sleep, a shortage of money, improper clothing for the day's events, or a stuffy nose.

You begin speaking negative words, preconditioning yourself for things to go wrong all day long. Sure enough, they do!

Take decisive action to prevent this from happening. Resist it with a shot of antihistamine. Turn your speech against Satan: Tell him you refuse to have a bad day or give in to emotion. Quote Scripture. It will only take a few minutes. Declare how much you have to be thankful for. Count your blessings.

A spirit of thankfulness is a form of resistance to Satan and to depression.

You can offset feelings of inadequacy or avert a "pity party" by thanksgiving.

Depression results in heaviness. When a spirit tries to stamp out your desire to be normal, do what Isaiah says: Exchange the garment of praise for the spirit of heaviness. (Is. 61:3.)

Guidelines for Resisting Depression

1. Stop blaming others for *your* feelings. (Your feelings will change.)

2. Check your priorities. Put the important ones first.

3. Try to spot the cause of your insecurities. It could be a carry-over from childhood.

4. Evaluate your losses. If a loss is causing your depression, it may not be important.

5. When you feel a low time coming, stay active.

6. Even though you may not feel like it, speak loud words of praise and victory. Vocal expression dominates feelings.

7. Triumphantly read aloud a large portion of Scripture.

8. Be selective with whom you share. You need strength, not sympathy.

9. Pray in the Spirit a great deal.

10. When your thoughts start turning toward yourself, do something quickly for someone else.

7
Overeating

I press toward the mark for the prize of the high calling of God in Christ Jesus.

Brethren, be followers together of me, and mark them which walk so as ye have us for an ensample.

(For·many walk, of whom I have told you often, and now tell you even weeping, that they are the enemies of the cross of Christ:

Whose end is destruction, whose God is their belly, and whose glory is in their shame, who mind earthly things.)

Philippians 3:14, 17-19

The Apostle Paul, one of the greatest men of history, invites the believer to live as he did. He was probably not obese; he may have even been gaunt.

Paul's concern was for a fine line. One can press toward the mark for the prize of the high calling or take part in the actions of the Lord's enemies who mind earthly things, making a god of their bellies.

Paul is writing about a very high priority: Earthly things are not supposed to rule us. In Romans 12:1 he states:

I beseech you therefore, brethren, by the mercies of God, that ye present your bodies a living sacrifice, holy, acceptable unto God, which is your reasonable service ("spiritual worship" AMP).

Learn to Control the Body

Resisting the desire to overeat is not a popular subject. The body has its own mind and appetite. The Bible calls uncontrolled appetite "lust."

Most overweight Christians have heard more than enough sermons on overeating. They don't need lectures;

they need help. They genuinely want to solve the problem and have usually tried every weight loss plan available.

Resisting food, especially saying "no" to sweets, is often one of the most difficult things for the average Christian to do. Counting calories is not an effective solution. The only way to successfully control weight is to learn how to rule your body rather than letting it rule you.

The Unredeemed Body

The bodies of those who are born again will not be redeemed until the rapture or resurrection. The body is not Christian; it is only an earthly house in which we live while on earth. Paul said, *It is sown in corruption; it is raised in incorruption* (1 Cor. 15:42); *It is sown a natural body; it is raised a spiritual body* (v. 44). Most backslidden Christians have somehow allowed their appetites to dominate them.

Once when I was on a trip to visit some churches in the Midwest, I became aware that my body not only had its own appetite but its own voice.

I was driving along one afternoon and, a little sleepy, needed a break. Knowing of an ice cream parlor a short distance up the road, I began to think about a milk shake. The more I thought about it, the more my body began to plead for it.

Suddenly I realized my body was about to dominate me! I resisted by driving past the ice cream stand and saying, "No, body, you're not going to get that milk shake!" My body reacted by pleading so hard I almost turned the car around and went back.

I am not overweight and could have enjoyed that milk shake without endangering my health. (In fact, I do allow myself to have one occasionally.)

Jesus said, *It is written, Man shall not live by bread alone, but by every word that proceedeth out of the mouth of God* (Matt. 4:4). He did not forbid me from eating bread (or cake!). He just warned that bread was not all man should eat. The mouth was made for more than just food and drink.

Being a little overweight will not kill you. My reason for resisting my body when it demanded the milk shake was not weight control. Paul said that we are to present our bodies a living sacrifice. Our bodies do not present *us*.

If I had given in to the demands of my body, it would have dominated me. My body would enjoy a milk shake three times a day if I were to let it. Paul is saying, "Christian, control your body!" If the corrupted body is not resisted, it will have its way.

Discipline Brings Happiness

God calls sweets *dainties* or *deceitful meats*:

When thou sittest to eat with a ruler, consider diligently what is before thee:

And put a knife to thy throat, if thou be a man given to appetite.

Be not desirous of his dainties: for they are deceitful meat.

Proverbs 23:1-3

Is God taking all the fun out of living in our physical bodies? No! Learn a great truth: Your life is happier when the flesh is denied. The uncontrolled body becomes pampered, spoiled, lazy, and rebellious. When it eats all it wants, especially delicacies, it is unhappy. (See Chapter 13.)

A person who has just lost twenty pounds has a smile and a bright expression on his face. If you run into the same person six months later and discover that he has regained all the weight, his smile won't be the same. He will be frustrated inside.

A glow emanates from the inner man of one who denies lustful appetite and exercises control. One who surrenders that control reflects frustration, depression, and guilt. He loses self-esteem.

When you begin saying no to your appetite for food or any other desire of the flesh, you begin gaining mastery over your body. Not only will your body become healthier and more beautiful, but you will have discovered the secret to happy, successful living! **The key to happiness is discipline.**

The next time you are offered a calorie-loaded delicacy, say, "No, thank you," even if your hand is reaching out to take it.

Gluttony, A Form of Rebellion

And they shall say unto the elders of his city, This our son is stubborn and rebellious, he will not obey our voice; he is a glutton, and a drunkard.

And all the men of his city shall stone him with stones, that he die: so shalt thou put evil away from among you; and all Israel shall hear, and fear.

Deuteronomy 21:20,21

One of the words used in this passage to describe the son's rebellion was *gluttony*. For this he was to be stoned! I am not recommending such severe treatment, but I am pointing out that gluttony is rebellion against God.

Control your physical appetite in the same way you control Satan—resist. Resist that appetite with inner spiritual resolve. Show yourself (and Satan!) that you are in control of your body.

Sometimes you have to make your body raise its hands and cooperate in worship. At those times you are presenting your body as a living sacrifice. Take authority and dominion over your body; even use the name of Jesus to make it conform to your will. When you keep your body under control, you will find it easier to cut down on your food consumption.

8
Pride

The wicked in his pride doth persecute the poor: let them be taken in the devices that they have imagined.

Psalm 10:2

Thou hast rebuked the proud that are cursed . . . .

Psalm 119:21

When pride cometh, then cometh shame.
Proverbs 11:2

Pride goeth before destruction, and an haughty spirit before a fall.

Proverbs 16:18

An high look, and a proud heart, and the plowing of the wicked, is sin.

Proverbs 21:4

Seest thou a man wise in his own

conceit? there is more hope of a fool than of him.

Proverbs 26:12

He that is of a proud heart stirreth up strife . . . .

Proverbs 28:25

In Mark 7:21-23, we see that Jesus names pride along with adultery and murder as being evil. We saw in Proverbs 6 that pride is the number one thing God hates. He openly reveals His punishment of those caught in it: *A man's pride shall bring him low . . .* (Prov. 29:23).

Pride caused the fall of King Nebuchadnezzar in ancient Babylon:

The king (Nebuchadnezzar) spake, and said, Is not this great Babylon, that I have built for the house of the kingdom by the might of my power, and for the honour of my majesty?

While the word was in the king's mouth, there fell a voice from heaven, saying, O king Nebuchadnezzar, to thee it is spoken;

The kingdom is departed from thee.
                              Daniel 4:30,31

King Nebuchadnezzar, driven from his royal palace, was made to live in the forest and eat grass like an ox. His hair grew like eagles' feathers and his nails like birds' claws. (v. 33.)

Not until he came to himself and gave praise to God did complete sanity, health, and his kingdom return to him. (vv. 34-37.)

This story reveals the cause, punishment, and remedy for pride. Because God *usually* blesses and prospers us slowly, we sometimes forget our former position. Pride creeps in slowly.

When David first became king, he was humble. God blessed him, giving him victory after victory until the whole kingdom was reestablished under his rule. Because of God's blessing, David began thinking he could do no wrong. Pride crept in. He sinned with

Bathsheba and murdered her husband. For that he was harshly punished.

Pride has caused many successful pastors and evangelists to fall. Sometimes it results from overspending and overbuilding to make a name for themselves. God blessed them, but they allowed pride to get in the way of common sense and sound business practices.

Effects of Pride

Pride causes a person to become unteachable. Because he feels he no longer needs advice, he quits listening to the counsel of his peers. Then false doctrine can creep in undetected.

Pride causes a person to commit the sin of presumption, *the great transgression* (Ps. 19:13). This sin is seldom understood.

Sometimes people pray for things far beyond their faith. They are often merely feeding their egos.

A minister needs to be very careful when presenting a message of "name it and claim it." Otherwise it can be misleading. A few successes can stir up pride in a Christian who was previously humble and satisfied with his material possessions. The thought of having instant riches had never before crossed his mind. Suddenly things became a substitute for relationship.

God is good and desires to bless and prosper His people. But He will do it in the right way at the proper time.

In his epistle James gives an excellent warning about pride and presumption:

Go to now, ye that say, To day or to morrow we will go into such a city, and continue there a year, and buy and sell, and get gain:

Whereas you know not what shall be on the morrow . . .

For that ye ought to say, If the Lord will, we shall live, and do this, or that.
                                        James 4:13-15

As we have seen, James 4:7 says, *Submit yourselves therefore to God. Resist the devil, and he will flee from you.* Verse ten tells us how to resist pride: *Humble yourselves in the sight of the Lord, and he shall lift you up.*

This verse provides the answer to most of the backlash caused by people listening to great Bible teaching and hearing only what they want to hear!

Prefacing every petition in prayer with ''if it be Thy will'' is wrong when we know what God's will is. But it is not wrong to have a spirit of humility by being ever ready to submit the human will to the superseding will of God.

God always has a higher will for us. It can easily be His will for us to have a better paying job, a new house, or a better car. However, it is not His will for us to become proud or feel superior to others who do not have the good things we have received.

God's Highest Will

God's highest will and law is for us to have humble hearts and to have every need supplied. Can you live in an expensive home, drive a $30,000 car, and be even more modest and humble than when you lived in a one-bedroom home and drove an old rattletrap? If so, then you are a good prospect for God's best!

Catch James' spirit. He is not against going to a city to buy and sell and get gain; he is against boasting about it. He is not against ''naming it and claiming it'' as long as the thing claimed is in God's will.

James is emphasizing that the highest goal is having God's perfect will in our lives in everything we say and do.

He makes his point very clear when he says, *Ye ask, and receive not, because ye ask amiss* (with the wrong motive), *that ye may consume it upon your lusts* (James 4:3).

He tells of God's merciful and kind nature seen in the way He dealt with Job. *Behold, we count them happy which endure. Ye have heard of the patience of Job, and have seen the end of the Lord; that the Lord is very pitiful, and of tender mercy* (James 5:11). Job lost nearly everything, but God restored it twice over.

James' teaching does not contradict John's who wrote: *Beloved, I wish above all things that thou mayest prosper and be in health, even as thy soul prospereth* (3 John 2). If James were alive today, he would make the same statement.

God wants us to be blessed in every way. He also wants us to resist the devil and all evil, including pride—a great evil. Pride will bring you low, rob you of eternal values, and even kill you. God hates pride with a perfect vengeance.

False Pride

Some Christians have developed a false pride. They give the appearance of thinking they are better than the rest of the Christian world because they attend churches in which they can receive more than most churchgoers. Instead of being vain, they should be humbly thankful.

As a faith teacher, I must teach the whole Bible, all of its truths. I dare not pull back from declaring the whole counsel of God because some people abuse this wonderful message of *Jesus Christ the same yesterday, and to day, and for ever* (Heb. 13:8).

God wants His people to have prosperity, but not to be covetous and materially minded. We are not to resist the message of healing and prosperity, but *pride* over these things. Jesus equated pride with adultery and murder.

Be Thankful

The best way to resist pride is to continually speak words of praise and gratitude to God for what you have. Because you are a child of the King, you can live like a king with all the benefits of royalty. Just remember that your King was humble.

Don't judge someone who is not materially blessed as lacking in faith. Don't think, *He didn't get his answer to prayer because he doesn't know how to pray like I do.*

Someone has said that a proud Christian is more valuable to Satan than an atheist!

Constantly resist pride. The greater abundance of things that God gives you, the more you must resist the devil. When you do, he will flee and take pride with him.

9
Gossip

Thou shalt not go up and down as a talebearer among thy people: neither shalt thou stand against the blood of thy neighbour: I am the Lord.

Leviticus 19:16

A talebearer revealeth secrets: but he that is of a faithful spirit concealeth the matter.

Proverbs 11:13

A froward man soweth strife: and a whisperer separateth chief friends.

Proverbs 16:28

The words of a talebearer are as wounds, and they go down into the innermost parts of the belly.

Proverbs 18:8

Where no wood is, there the fire goeth out: so where there is no talebearer, the strife ceaseth.

When he (the talebearer) *speaketh fair, believe him not: for there are seven abominations in his heart.*

Proverbs 26:20,25

For we hear that there are some which walk among you disorderly, working not at all, but are busybodies.

2 Thessalonians 3:11

Gossip is devastating to both the talebearer and the hearer:

And withal they learn to be idle, wandering about from house to house; and not only idle, but tattlers also and busybodies, speaking things which they ought not.

For some are already turned aside after Satan.

1 Timothy 5:13,15

But let none of you suffer as a murderer, or as a thief, or as an evildoer, or as a busybody in other men's matters.

> 1 Peter 4:15

Resisting the desire to gossip (bear tales, whisper, spread rumors) is one of our toughest assignments as Christians.

Gossip is common in the social world. Once people come to know the Lord, they carry this habit into the fellowship of the saints.

At the Judgment it will be staggering to hear of the damage done by this satanic weapon. Gossip is behind every church split and ruined ministry.

The Seven Abominations

Even if what a gossiper says seems to be of merit, place no credibility in it. The gossiper lays up deceit within him and has seven abominations in his heart. (Prov. 26:24,25.)

Most likely a list of those abominations would include the following:

1. Murder

Gossipers murder not with a gun, but with the tongue. With their idle conversation, they murder the reputations of honest people. Talebearers even drive some of these people to suicide.

On Judgment Day what will God say to the talebearer who has caused the death of another person? Because Satan is a liar and murderer, whoever listens to him commits the same acts.

2. Theft

Few gossipers would shoplift, but they never think twice about picking up the phone and robbing someone else of his reputation.

3. Strife

Strife is an insidious abomination because gossipers do not initiate it; they just keep it going! They may even feel innocent of any evildoing because they speak the gossip in the form of a prayer request. Just one comment or question may be enough to keep strife-causing rumors boiling.

4. Revenge

The word itself is abominable. The vengeful person says, ''Because I have suffered, you will also suffer! If you tell anything that I've done, I'll tell everything bad about you that I can think of!''

Satan's fury against God and the Church is fed by revenge. Don't be party to it. If you suffer, do it alone.

Vengeance is mine; I will repay, saith the Lord (Rom. 12:19). God will vindicate the right. All sin will be found out and reproved by Him. God is the judge, not us.

5. Exaggeration

Exaggeration is evil especially when someone makes a small mistake sound serious by blowing it out of proportion. Someone who intentionally exaggerates to damage another person's reputation commits a horrible evil. If it is absolutely necessary to relate something negative about a person, determine to downplay it as much as possible while still being factual.

6. Lying

This is the worst abomination because it comes from the lord of lies, Satan, performing at his best. Often a person knows what he hears is a lie; but instead of checking its validity, he passes it on. By doing that he becomes just as much a liar as the person who first told it.

God hates lying. Revelation 21:8 says, . . . *all liars, shall have their part in the lake which burneth with fire and brimstone . . . .*

7. Unhappiness

This abomination is camouflaged. Because happy people have so many good things to talk about, they are not likely to gossip. Their conversations are about positive rather than negative things. They have no desire to wound anyone. Socially well adjusted and happily serving their Lord, they don't have time to be busybodies.

The happier you become in your joy of living for Jesus, the less time you will have to take part in gossip about other people.

The seven abominations should inspire us to help each other by refusing to gossip.

Guidelines for Resisting Gossip

Aid yourself in resisting the tendency to gossip by doing these things:

1. **When you hear gossip, name it as such.** If you do not consciously recognize it, you will pass it along more easily.

2. **When a person tells you something about someone else, ask yourself, "Is this hearsay or fact?"**

   Do not pass along hearsay as the truth. Check all of the facts and hear both sides of the story before you believe it.

   When you let the enemy use your tongue to spread hearsay about the weaknesses of others, you are weakening the Kingdom of God and doing damage to a brother or sister with whom you intend to spend eternity.

3. **Search for ways of correcting the gossiper.** Ask him, "Where did you get your information? How do you know it's true?" If you know the person is spreading gossip, you are obligated to make him aware that Satan is using him.

   Say this, "Instead of talking about this person, let's bow our heads and pray for him."

You should pray something like this:

Heavenly Father, we thank You for (name the person). *We know You love him and that Christ died for him. Help us to love him by keeping this to ourselves. May his name never be mentioned by us again, except in prayer or in a Christ-like manner. Amen.*

If all of us who use the name of Jesus resist gossip and gossipers, the total Body of Christ can be filled with the "antihistamine" to defeat this deadly sin.

10
Sickness

Bless the Lord, O my soul, and forget not all his benefits: who forgiveth all thine iniquities; who healeth all thy diseases.

Psalm 103:2,3

. . . I will put (permit) none of these diseases upon thee, which I have brought (permitted) upon the Egyptians: for I am the Lord that healeth thee.

Exodus 15:26

Pleasant words are as an honeycomb, sweet to the soul, and health to the bones.

Proverbs 16:24

Surely he hath borne our griefs (sicknesses), and carried our sorrows (diseases) . . . and with his stripes we are healed.

Isaiah 53:4,5

Heal me, O Lord, and I shall be healed; save me, and I shall be saved: for thou art my praise.

Jeremiah 17:14

When the even was come, they brought unto him many that were possessed with devils: and he cast out the spirits with his word, and healed all that were sick:

That it might be fulfilled which was spoken by Esaias (Isaiah) *the prophet, saying, Himself took our infirmities, and bare our sicknesses.*

Matthew 8:16,17

But if the Spirit of him that raised up Jesus from the dead dwell in you, he that raised up Christ from the dead shall also quicken your mortal (liable to death) *bodies by his Spirit that dwelleth in you.*

Romans 8:11

These Scripture verses and many others teach us of God's concern for our physical bodies, the temples of His Holy Spirit.

For two thousand years, the clergy has misled the Church concerning God's attitude toward physical healing. Jesus went about doing good and healing **all** that were oppressed of the devil. (Acts 10:38.) This alone should show us the Father's attitude toward all physical suffering.

When Satan introduced sin into the world, along with death he also brought in sickness and disease. Disease and suffering in the form of germs and viruses constantly surround us. We must take the spiritual antihistamine of resistance as medicine to ward off sickness.

Resist With Words

While we are here on earth, we want to serve the Lord with vigor and physical strength. The average Christian has never been taught about the healing heritage that belongs to him. Instead of resisting sickness, he claims it! He says: ''I am coming down with a cold." "The flu season is here—looks like I'll be coming down with it soon." "I don't feel well. I guess I'll be sick in bed tomorrow." "Cancer runs in my family, so I'll probably have it someday."

Read what the Bible says about the use of your tongue:

Death and life are in the power of the tongue: and they that love it shall eat the fruit thereof.

Proverbs 18:21

He that hath knowledge spareth his words: and a man of understanding is of an excellent ("cool" AMP) *spirit.*

Even a fool, when he holdeth his peace (tongue), *is counted wise: and he that shutteth his lips is esteemed a man of understanding.*

Proverbs 17:27,28

A wise Christian will not negate with his mouth what Jesus purchased for him with His stripes.

Resistance comes from a strong attitude. One must set his will against receiving sickness and symptoms.

A young lady named Karen, able to move only with great painful effort, was told by the doctors that she had rheumatoid arthritis. They said she would be an invalid the rest of her life.

Karen and her husband set themselves in agreement to resist the disease. They resisted it in both attitude and word. Believing, they confessed the Word daily.

After a year of persistence, the spiritual "antihistamine" did the job! Karen received almost total healing. She gave birth to a daughter, and is happily serving the Lord in her church.

God Does Not Make Us Sick

The majority of Christians have been led to believe that God is trying to teach them something through their suffering. The kind of suffering the

Bible teaches comes from living a godly life, one that brings persecution because of consecration.

A house divided against itself cannot stand. (Mark 3:25.) If we believe that God makes us sick so that He can heal us, we would also have to believe that God makes us commit sin so that He can save us!

Both by word and example Jesus teaches that Satan is the culprit. (John 10:10.) Jesus came to destroy Satan's works, both sin and sickness.

Guidelines for Resisting Sickness

Resisting Satan will weaken him. When symptoms of sickness or disease try to attack you, do these things:

1. Resist with a firm, loud voice. Tell Satan to leave you alone in the name of Jesus!

2. Memorize the Word pertinent to your healing *before* you get sick!

3. If you become sick suddenly, have a believer lay hands on you according to Mark 16:18.

4. If you do become sick, turn to God before you consult medical doctors. We thank God for medical science, but we must follow the order given in James 5:14 to *first* seek anointing and prayer.

5. If you are alone when sickness strikes, phone a fellow believer and ask him to agree with you for healing. (Matt. 18:19.)

Most Christians don't follow these five steps. Every pastor should have the people in the congregation come forward to be anointed with oil and prayed for in at least one service each week. This will give them something to look forward to when symptoms strike.

Jesus told the disciples, *The thief (Satan) cometh not, but for to steal, and to kill, and to destroy: I am come that they might have life, and that they might have it more abundantly* (John 10:10).

Abundant life is not automatic. You receive it after you act in faith to resist the works of Satan and to receive the finished work of the Cross.

The New Testament Church began with great miracles and healings. This church age will end as it began—*by miracles and wonders and signs* (Acts 2:22). Get ready to be part of this great move!

11
Weak Times

And Jesus being full of the Holy Ghost returned from Jordan, and was led by the Spirit into the wilderness,

Being forty days tempted of the devil. And in those days he did eat nothing: and when they were ended, he afterward hungered.

And the devil said unto him . . . .
Luke 4:1-3

In this passage we see how Jesus was tempted by Satan at a very weak time. All of us experience times of stress and strain. Satan waits for those times in order to tempt us.

Even the great men and women of faith in the Bible experienced weakness and temptation.

When King David greatly sinned, it was at a weak time in his life. As a young man he never knew defeat; even when he ran from Saul, he had victory. When he stopped going to battle and began sitting idle, he fell foolishly into sin and paid dearly for this.

Moses, weakened by the criticism of the children of Israel, lost his temper in a tense moment and smote the rock. Because of his action, he was denied the privilege of entering the Promised Land of Canaan. (Num. 20:11,12.)

The strong Samson, weakened by his fiance's continual nagging, revealed the secret of his might. As a result, he lost his power and his life. (Judg. 16:16,17.)

As Solomon grew older, he clouded his relationship with God by surrounding himself with beautiful women from many countries. (1 Kings 11:1-4.) At this time of weakness, he fell into indulgence. Because of his unfaithfulness to God, his kingdom began to fall apart.

History books are full of stories about strong men and women who have fallen during times of weakness.

A Strength Can Become A Weakness

One of the great paradoxes of the human character is that a person's strength can become his weakness.

Moses was meek. In a time of stress this became his weakness when he lost his temper and smote the rock.

In a time of temptation, David's integrity of heart became his weakness when his heart led him into adultery and murder.

Overconfident because of his strength, Samson became easy prey for the wiles of a beautiful woman.

When Solomon failed to exercise wisdom in choosing his wives, his wisdom became his weakness.

Peter's boldness led him into trouble at the high priest's palace. In his time of weakness, he cursed and denied his Lord. (Luke 22:56,60.)

Identify your strength, then claim and exercise added resistance so that it will not become your weakness. Be on guard lest Satan tempt you into failure through the very thing in which you feel most confident.

If your strength is your great moral integrity, don't trust it in a severe test. Never let yourself be alone with a member of the opposite sex when something damaging to your Christian experience might happen. This wisdom becomes our antihistamine of resistance.

If people have trusted you with their secrets, you have a great responsibility. It would be better for you never to have had that kind of ministry if there is the slightest danger that you might betray someone's confidence in a time of weakness.

If you have always been true to your mate, don't allow your mind to think about how attractive another person is.

If you are holy in thought, beware of anything that might cause impure thinking.

If you have walked not as a part of this world but in holiness, be careful of what you allow yourself to read and watch on television.

If you have never been tempted to commit adultery, refuse to read pornographic material.

If you have never stolen or coveted, avoid talking about wanting things you don't have.

If you have always successfully prayed for and received the things you have needed, don't reach beyond your faith in presumptive prayer.

Prepare Yourself For Weak Times

Couples who have been happily married for a number of years should know to recognize each other's weak times. They should use more caution, being quick to forgive and careful to hold their tongues.

We all have areas in which we are less skilled than others. It is wisdom to refrain from pointing those out in each other.

The man who reminds his wife that she can't cook as well as his mother does not help her become a better cook. It might get him a burned supper instead!

A woman who reminds her husband that he is not the handyman her father is does not help him become a skilled mechanic. It might instead provoke him into "fixing" a few things around the house that don't need fixing!

Exercise resistance about opening your mouth when someone else is having a low time. "I told you so" should never be spoken.

During your own weak times, exercise resistance about speaking what you think. If you are at the time of life when chemical changes are taking place in your body, use more resistance against becoming depressed or irritable.

If you failed to mold your children during their formative years, don't try to make up for it by scolding and nagging them once they have become teenagers.

If your loved one is determined to make what you consider to be a mistake, stay with him. If he is right, he will need your support to see it through. If he is wrong, he will need you even more. By refusing to support him in his decision, you may lose him entirely. This especially holds true if your son or daughter decides to marry someone of whom you do not approve.

Use more resistance during the low times of the month. Mondays are low for some people. If they are for you, prepare yourself. Use more resistance against feeling sorry for yourself or speaking negative things.

Resist the temptation to "correct" others. Have the courtesy and sense to ask before you offer advice!

When you feel physically low, do more spiritually. When you are becoming "so heavenly minded that you are no earthly good," do more physically.

Don't become discouraged, envious, or bitter when you hear of other people's successes, especially when it seems as though you never succeed. Resist by saying, "I am happy for them, and my time is coming!"

12
Resisting In Faith

Casting all your care (worries) upon him; for he careth for you.

Be sober, be vigilant; because your adversary the devil, as a roaring lion, walketh about, seeking whom he may devour:

Whom resist steadfast in the faith, knowing that the same afflictions are accomplished in your brethren that are in the world.

1 Peter 5:7-9

Be ye angry, and sin not: let not the sun go down upon your wrath:

Neither give place to the devil.

Ephesians 4:26,27

Put on the whole armour of God, that ye

may be able to stand against the wiles of the devil.

Ephesians 6:11

Often Christians find themselves able to resist the devil for only short periods of time. A common remark is, "Even though I have resisted with all my might, nothing seems any better." When they try to resist food, they give in after just a few meals.

Some Christians who are able to resist gossiping for a while catch themselves doing it again.

"I tried to control my mind, but just couldn't do it," say some men who cannot think pure thoughts about ladies.

People able to resist depression briefly say that sooner or later it gets the best of them and they end up having a prolonged "pity party."

Why do so many people who try hard to resist Satan's attacks fail so miserably when it comes to self-control?

Trying your best not to do something is not good enough. Human will power alone cannot resist a spiritual enemy. You must resist in faith, using the powerful weapons of the Spirit.

"That's easy to say," someone might remark. "But how do I do it?"

Besides our faith, we have another powerful weapon at our disposal: our **imaginations.**

Develop Your Spiritual Imagination

Because of habit, we tend to picture negative things like failure and defeat. We dream up unrealistic fantasies or let our fears suggest terrible things that could happen.

Put your imagination to work *for* you, instead of *against* you, by using it to call up positive images of the way you want things to be. Your imagination should be the blueprint from which you build your dream.

First Peter 5:9 declares that the world has the same afflictions (trials and tests) that we have. The people in the world are also looking for work, trying to lose weight, and seeking escape from depression. They face the same things we face, and more. But we Christians have a weapon the world does not have: faith.

Why should the Christian be any less optimistic and confident than a person in the world? The Christian's new mind, his born-again spirit, will work for him if he lets it.

Before you begin trying to achieve a goal, prepare your faith and imagination first.

Faith Knows

Be still, and know that I am God (Ps. 46:10) is often quoted, but seldom acted upon. The Scriptures repeatedly admonish us to wait upon God, to spend time with Him.

The key word to having faith is *know*. We are rarely still (waiting on God) long enough to "know" that the thing we have asked for is already ours.

In Mark 11:24 Jesus taught us: *Therefore . . . whatever you ask for in prayer, believe that you have received it, and it will be yours* (NIV[15]).

Just claiming something with positive talk will not bring a miracle. Resisting unbelief by speaking and **believing** the Word is what brings victory.

With your spiritual imagination, you must see yourself possessing the desired thing *before* you confess that you have it.

If you want to lose weight, imagine looking at your new trim figure in the mirror. Imagine hearing other people say how good you look.

If you need employment, picture yourself busy at the job you want.

You cannot see one quick picture and receive the manifestation. Possibly someone who has developed a deep relationship with the Lord by serving and waiting on Him for years can do this, but not the average Christian.

It will take time to develop your spiritual imagination.

When I needed an airplane for my ministry, I spent months in preparation before I felt ready in my spirit to ask in faith for it. After agreeing with a fellow believer that I had the plane, I began imagining myself flying it. My prayer was answered just a few weeks later.

Look back at the times when your faith has worked. You will recall that you were applying these faith principles.

Add to Your Faith and Use It

Faith alone will not stand the test;

we need to add to it and strengthen it. Peter tells us some things we need to add to our faith: virtue, knowledge, temperance, patience, godliness, brotherly kindness, and charity. (2 Pet. 1:5-8.) James reminds us that *faith, if it hath not works, is dead, being alone* (James 2:17).

We must do something with our faith: we must keep it. (2 Tim. 4:7.) In order to keep it, we must resist unbelief, which is evil and thrives in a negative environment. Unbelief cannot stand before simple faith; don't give in to it.

A Confession of Faith

God blesses me when I am coming in and going out. He will meet all my needs when I seek Him first.

Faith accepts the promise and sees the fruit, waits on God until it knows, and never struggles—it rests.

According to 1 John 5:14,15 I have the petitions that I have desired of God.

I resist doubt and fear, the enemies of my faith.

I resist the devil and, through the eyes of faith, see him running from me, taking his baggage with him!

This is the victory, even my faith. (1 John 5:4.) The victory is mine!

13
Joy,
The Best Antihistamine

A merry heart doeth good like a medi-cine: but a broken spirit drieth the bones.

Proverbs 17:22

For the kingdom of God is not meat and drink; but righteousness, and peace, and joy in the Holy Ghost.

For he that in these things serveth Christ is acceptable to God, and approved of men.

Romans 14:17,18

Rejoice in the Lord alway: and again I say, Rejoice.

Philippians 4:4

When the Apostle Paul wrote to the Philippian church and told them to rejoice in the Lord always, he was instructing them to take the best medicine possible for resistance against every attack of the enemy.

Joy is the best resistance against: disease in a body; dissention and divorce in a home; discord and disharmony in a church.

A Happy Heart

A young man who had just undergone a heart transplant told me of his experience. This operation was his last hope.

The young man expressed his gratitude to God for this extension of his life, especially since there had been other patients waiting for heart donors.

The body was created to immediately reject any foreign object introduced into it. A patient can receive a perfectly healthy heart which performs as expected until the body sends its killer forces to destroy the foreign organ. The recipient body rejects the very thing that is keeping it alive.

I discussed with the young man this well-known danger and asked him if there had been any major medical breakthrough to help the body receive the new organ.

"Yes," he answered. "I will be one of the first heart transplant patients to take a new medication to treat this problem. The drug is a suppressant which keeps the new heart happy."

Webster's Dictionary defines a "suppressant" as "a substance which lowers the rate of muscular or nervous activity."

"Are you telling me that the physical body will not reject this happy heart?" I asked.

"That's exactly how the doctors explained it to me," he answered.

Immediately I thought of an important parallel. The main reason a new Christian often backslides is that the unredeemed physical body sets out to reject the new, happy, born-again heart.

A new Christian who is happy in serving the Lord Jesus Christ won't leave the Church. But if Satan or circumstances cause the new convert to become discouraged and lose his joy, he stops doing the things necessary to keep his new faith living and growing.

Sometimes he loses his joy because he still has not solved a problem he faced before being born again. Sometimes he loses it when he mingles with unhappy Christians who gossip. The way the person loses his joy is not as important as the fact that he allows himself to be robbed of it.

Isaiah 12:3 says, *Therefore with joy shall ye draw water out of the wells of salvation.* No one but you can joyfully draw the eternal water for you.

We have certain duties to perform. We are to gather with the saints, lift our hands in worship to God, pay the tithe, witness to others, pray, and read the Bible. We are to do these things with great joy, and we are responsible for our *own* joy.

If you lose your joy, the enemy can rob you of your salvation.

Proverbs 17:22 says, *A merry heart doeth good like a medicine: but a broken spirit drieth the bones.* Leviticus 17:11 tells us that *the life of the flesh is in the blood.* The blood flowing through our physical bodies is the source of our health. It fights off viruses and infections. Healthy blood comes from healthy, happy bones. When the bones are unhappy, they dry up.

Ana the Lord shall guide thee continually, and satisfy thy soul in drought, and make fat thy bones: and thou shalt be like a watered garden, and like a spring of water, whose waters fail not.

Then shalt thou delight thyself in the Lord; and I will cause thee to ride upon the high places of the earth, and feed thee with the heritage of Jacob thy father: for the mouth of the Lord hath spoken it.

Isaiah 58:11,14

Maintain Your Joy

When we trust in the Lord and keep ourselves joyful, we are practicing the best preventative medicine known to man.

These thoughts will help you develop and maintain a spirit of joy:

1. Even when you don't feel like it, make yourself laugh.

2. Even though you feel like frowning, make yourself smile.

3. When another person speaks negatively, think of something positive to say.

4. Laugh loudly at a good joke.

5. Memorize funny things and relate them.

6. Be a collector of good jokes.

7. Even though you may have heard the joke, laugh with the person who is telling it.

8. Go to church in joyful expectancy.

9. Worship and praise joyfully.

10. Pay your tithes and give offerings joyfully.

A healthy church is happy. The congregation of a happy church quickly responds to funny stories. An unhappy church is stagnant. Its subdued, dejected-looking people are reluctant to even enter into worship. In my extensive travels, I have been in hundreds of churches and have never seen a growing church that has a sad, unhappy congregation.

The pastor of a dynamic, thriving church is quick to laugh and express his joy. His face usually glows with an attitude of faith and trust both in God and people.

The successful pastor must resist losing his joy. This is the day of great revival and a day when the churches are filled with happy worshipers. *Thou meetest him that rejoiceth* (Is. 64:5) can apply to an entire church.

Medical science acknowledges that the best resistance to disease is a healthy body and confirms the therapeutic effect of laughter. One medical scientist defines laughter as "stationary jogging," because the muscles and blood pressure react in such a healthy way during laughter. After laughter subsides, the body benefits from its relaxed state.

Some anthropologists believe that laughter evolved from primitive man's expression of triumph over a defeated foe. Thus laughter and joy signify to Satan that we stand against him in firm resistance.

Remember, *The joy of the Lord is your strength* (Neh. 8:10). The Word of God, the joy of the Lord, is the Christian's antihistamine.

Summary

Resisting, the Christian's anti-histamine, is far more valuable than one can surmise.

Those who have not resisted have a style of life that gives in to the enemy. They do not control their speech as they should, and they usually do not try to change. They will say, "It might work for some. But when I'm sick, I'm sick! When I'm low, I'm low!"

Even many pastors have made fun of the positive faith message. We hear things such as, "He is one of those 'name it and claim it' people. Don't ask him how he feels. He'll just quote Scripture."

Not only are we correct to teach this positive, Scripturally based faith message, but the latest medical studies prove correct in teaching people to deny rather than to claim. One leading psychiatrist studied the effect of denial on heart attack victims. He found that those who play down their illness may be more likely to survive a serious ailment. After studying 89 men during their hospital stays, he found that the denier was more likely to survive his stay than the patient who was full of fear and anxiety.

It seems that a strong resistance instead of a weak acquiescence can be of the same benefit as going to your doctor for a shot of antihistamine.

Resist and keep on resisting!

Deny and become a denier!

References

[1] W. E. Vine, *An Expository Dictionary of New Testament Words* (Old Tappan: Fleming H. Revell, 1966), p. 286.

[2] Joseph Henry Thayer, *A Greek-English Lexicon of the New Testament* by Grimm-Wilke (Grand Rapids: Zondervan Publishing House, 1963), p. 651.

[3] Arndt Gingrich, *A Greek-English Lexicon of the New Testament* (Grand Rapids: Zondervan Publishing House, 1957), p. 863.

[4] Liddell and Scott, *Greek-English Lexicon* (Oxford at the Clarendon Press, 1843), p. 1925.

[5] W. E. Vine, *Expository Dictionary*, Vol. II, p. 107.

[6] *The New English Bible* (New York: Oxford University Press and Cambridge University Press, 1962), p. 394.

[7] *The Expositor's Greek Testament* (Grand Rapids: W. B. Eerdmans Publishers, 1961), p. 460.

[8]James Strong, *The Exhaustive Concordance of the Bible* (Nashville: Abingdon, 1978), Greek Dictionary, p. 12.

[9]E. W. Bullinger, *A Critical Text Concordance to the English and Greek New Testament* (Grand Rapids: Zondervan Publishing House, 1975), p. 641.

[10]*Ellicott's Commentary on the Whole Bible* (Grand Rapids: Zondervan Publishing House, 1959), Vol. 8, p. 373.

[11]Adam Clarke, *Clarke's Commentary* (Nashville: Abingdon-Cokesbury Press), p. 820.

[12]R. C. H. Lenski, *Interpretation of the Epistle to the Hebrews and the Epistle of James* (Minneapolis: Augsburg Publishing House, 1961), p. 632.

[13]D. D. Whedan, *Commentary on the New Testament* (New York: Eaton and Mains, 1880), Section: Titus to Revelation, p. 178.

[14]W. E. Vine, *Expository Dictionary*, Vol. 4, p. 127.

[15]The New York International Bible Society, *The Holy Bible: New International Version* (Grand Rapids: Zondervan Bible Publishers, 1978), p. 939.

Roy H. Hicks is a successful minister of the Gospel who has given his life to pastoring and pioneering churches throughout the United States. He has served the Lord in various foreign  fields, having made missionary journeys to South America, the Orient, Australia, and New Zealand.

As a dedicated man of God, Dr. Hicks formerly served as General Supervisor of the Foursquare Gospel Churches and has become a popular speaker at charismatic conferences.

Perhaps the things that most endear Dr. Hicks to readers is his warmth and his ability to reach out as the true believer he is — a man of strong, positive faith, sharing a refreshing ministry through the power and anointing of the Holy Spirit.

To contact Dr. Hicks, write:

Dr. Roy H. Hicks
P. O. Box 4113
San Marcos, California 92069

Available From Harrison House Books By Dr. Roy H. Hicks